T0358783

fluffy flying
Seed

by Mary Auld

illustrations
by Dawn Cooper

consultant botanist
Josh Styles MSc

Here are tiny seeds drifting through the air.
They are the seeds from a dandelion plant,
and one of them is me.

*Flowering plants such as
dandelions make seeds.
A seed is a little package
that holds a baby plant.*

*The seed is protected by a hard
casing. It is attached to a fluffy
parachute, so it can be lifted and
carried by the wind.*

One by one we drop to the ground.
Some of us land in water. Some of us are
eaten by birds.

*Dandelion seeds blow away
from their parent plant on the
wind. This gives them space
to grow well.*

I am lucky. I land in a
grassy field—a perfect
place for me to grow.

Here I am starting to grow.
My taproot pushes down into the ground.
My leaves push upward.

A seed starts to grow after about two or three weeks in the ground.

The taproot pushes out of the seed's hard case.

The taproot is strong. It holds the dandelion plant in place.

Tiny hairlike strands reach out off the taproot. They take in wate and goodness fror the soil.

Here are my first leaves growing above the ground.

Small and green, they make my food so I can grow bigger. They just need air, water, and sunlight!

The dandelion uses the food energy to grow, and the oxygen is released into the air.

The leaves trap light energy from the sun. They use this to change the carbon dioxide and water into the plant's food and oxygen.

The first leaves push up. They take in carbon dioxide from the air through tiny holes. The carbon dioxide mixes with water from the roots.

Here I am, bigger, stronger, and tastier! My large, jagged leaves make lots of food for me and provide food for others.

The dandelion's leaf shape gives it its name—it comes from dent-de-lion, French for lion's tooth.

Lots of animals, from caterpillars to deer, feed on the leaves, but the dandelion can grow more of them.

Here I am starting to flower. It is spring and I have grown buds on tall, hollow stalks. Look at all my different parts.

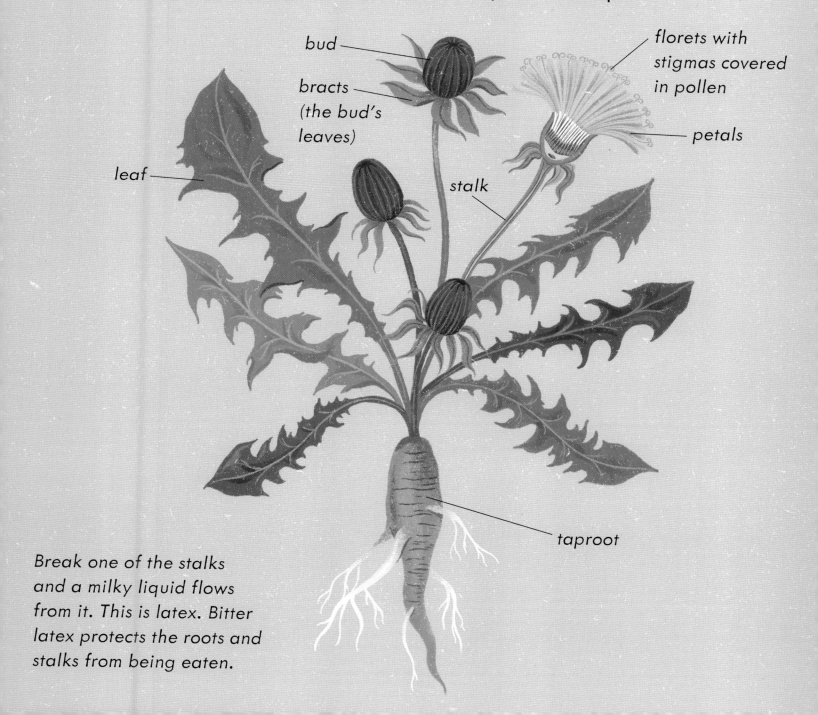

bud

bracts
(the bud's
leaves)

leaf

stalk

florets with
stigmas covered
in pollen

petals

taproot

Break one of the stalks
and a milky liquid flows
from it. This is latex. Bitter
latex protects the roots and
stalks from being eaten.

Here are my flowers. My buds have opened in the spring sunshine. My flower heads are like little suns! Bees buzz around them.

A dandelion's yellow petals surround a flower head made of around 100 tiny florets. These are tiny flowers.

Dandelion florets make nectar and pollen, food for insects, such as honeybees.

Dandelions are an important source of food for insects in the spring. Most other plants flower later in the year.

The night is falling. The sky is clear and it is frosty.
My flowers are closing up tight, safe from the cold.

Dandelion flower heads
close up when it gets dark.
The green bracts that
grow around the
flower protect it
from the cold.

The closed bracts keep
the nectar fresh and the
pollen dry inside the
flower—ready for the
insects in the morning.

Here is my meadow. It is full of dandelions and other flowers among the grasses.
The summer is arriving and the sunshine gives us the energy we need to grow.

A meadow is a habita shared by lots of plan and animals.

What insects can you see feeding on our nectar and pollen?

There are lots of animals, too, looking for food.

Animals can't make their own food. They eat plants or other animals that eat plants.

Swallows arrive in late spring. They feed on insects.

A rabbit nibbles on leaves, while the fox hopes to catch the rabbit.

Here I am making my seeds, and so are my plant friends around me. We make our seeds in different ways.

Many flowering plants make their seeds by pollination. This means that pollen from the flower of one plant must attach to the flower of another.

Insects, such as butterflies and bees, take clover pollen from flower to flower.

Grasses use wind to blow pollen from one plant to another.

Here are my flower heads, closing up, even though the sun is shining. Inside, my florets are changing. They are forming seeds.

Common dandelions usually form seeds inside their florets without pollination.

After a few days, a dandelion flower closes up for a week or more.

Its petals drop off, leaving wispy strands poking through the closed bracts.

Look at my flower heads now!

*When the bracts open again,
a magical transformation has
taken place.*

*Each floret has formed a
seed on a delicate, silky
pappus. Together, the
pappi form a ball shape.*

*The seed heads stay
open all the time.*

My golden-sun flower
has changed into a
fluffy full moon.

My seeds are ready,
and I wait for the
wind to carry them
away.

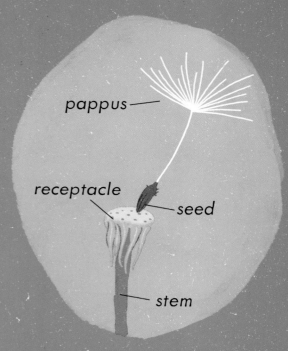

pappus

receptacle

seed

stem

The pappus is like a parachute.
Air flows through the ring of
tiny strands lifting the seed
up and away.

The seed is inside a hard,
jagged casing called
a capitulum.

Here are children. They each make a wish—and help me spread my seeds.

Dandelion seed heads can be called blowballs. Make a wish as you blow.

My fluffy pappi parachutes are amazing. Carried by the wind, they can take a seed far, far away from me.

Most dandelion seeds drop after a few yards but some travel long distances— as far as 50 miles.

A pappus's shape helps the seed land gently and upright on the ground, so it slips into the soil.

Look at my seedlings! Some have landed in people's gardens. Others are growing in unusual places. Dandelions are happy to grow almost anywhere.

Dandelions do well in people's gardens and farmers' fields . . .

. . . but they can grow in rocky or wasteland habitats.

Dandelions usually grow in temperate climates with four seasons, but can be found in mild temperate zones, such as around the Mediterranean Sea.